Rebecca R. Contreras 3/29/98

THE city of New Orleans is at the heart of world trade and has one of the busiest ports in the world. The Mississippi River provides a watery highway for huge ocean-going ships traveling the hundred miles from the Gulf of Mexico to the city's bustling piers.

It was the proximity to the Mississippi that prompted the French to settle here in a natural curve or crescent of the river in 1718. Since the city's earliest days, it has been the gateway to the vast Mississippi Valley. For many of its years, it has been one of America's largest cities, and today ranks among the continent's leading ports.

Although history runs deep in New Orleans, modern amenities like the Greater New

Orleans Bridge, a twin span connecting downtown with the West Bank, make the city easily accessible from the suburbs. Sleek skyscrapers grace the downtown skyline, creating a cosmopolitan atmosphere in keeping with one of America's modern metropolitan cities.

The multi-storied World Trade Center, at the foot of Canal Street, houses dozens of foreign consulates and international offices which keep New Orleans and America in touch with

all over the world arrive and depart. Beyond, the city spreads out in a gridiron pattern of streets bending with the curve of the river.

Fronting the World Trade Center is a tribute to New Orleans' unique history. In the Place de France, Joan of Arc sits astride her golden charger, prepared to lead her small force to victory over the English at Orleans in 1429. In British Park Place, statesman Winston Churchill is honored. Bernardo de Galvez, Spanish governor of Louisiana in the 1780's, guards the Spanish Plaza. The parks and statues represent the countries which contributed to the settlement and success of New Orleans and under whose flags it has resided.

Jackson Square, the heart of the French Quarter, is an island of green surrounded by the river, St. Louis Cathedral and the Pontalba Apartments, the oldest apartments in the country. The fascinating city of New Orleans fans out around it.

the world. A revolving gathering place on the 33rd floor of the center, called the Top of the Mart Lounge, offers a fascinating view of this unique city. As the lounge slowly revolves, visitors are treated to a spectacular birds-eye view of the city's blend of old and new. Spread below are Rivergate, the Exhibition Center, the New Orleans Convention Center, Spanish Plaza,'Riverwalk, Jax Brewery shopping plaza and the long wharves where cargo ships from

CANAL Street is the city's main downtown avenue. It runs from the Mississippi River to the shores of Lake Pontchartrain. The street is one of the most historic in New Orleans. Prior to the Louisiana Purchase, the Creoles (people descended from the first Spanish and French colonists) had settled in the French Quarter downriver of what is now Canal Street.

The upstart American settlers, not welcomed by the Creoles and not particularly fond of the relaxed lifestyle of the Creoles, preferred to settle on the upriver side and Canal Street became the dividing line. Each community had its own government and police force. The wide median strip in the center of the street became known as "neutral ground," site of occasional confrontations between the Creoles and newer residents.

Today, the animosity is forgotten but the median strips of the city's streets are still referred to as neutral ground.

The huge old building at the corner of Canal and Decatur streets is the Custom House. Taking up a whole city block, it

was built in 1894 and replaced Fort St. Louis which guarded the old French city. Once home to General Butler, commanding officer of the Union troops during Occupation in the Civil War, today it houses government offices. The building has identical entrances on all four sides because the builders couldn't decide which was to be the main entrance.

The foot of Canal Street was the site of the 1984 World's Fair. Today, you can catch the ferry at the foot of the street to Algiers across the river and explore Mardi Gras World, where parade floats are made. It's also a perfect place to catch the streetcar for an unforgettable tour of this delightful city.

On a more modern note, Canal Place, just up from the river, is a fashionable shopping complex with something to delight any shopper.

referred to as the Garden District and is aptly named. Beautifully land-scaped gardens surround many of the mansions, generally tucked behind lacy wrought iron fences and gates. The warm Louisiana weather provides the perfect atmosphere for an almost endless profusion of flowers the year round.

The perfect way to tour the Garden District is to hop aboard an historic streetcar to the area and begin a leisurely stroll at Prytania and Washington streets. The Rink, the South's first, built in the 1880's, has been converted into a shopping plaza. Stop for high tea at the coffee shop there.

Continue your tour along Coliseum and Second streets. Sadly, the histories of most of the wonderful homes in this district have been lost. Information about only a few is available. The Toby-Westfeldt

W HEN American settlers found themselves unwelcome in the French Quarter, they proceeded to build their elegant antebellum homes in an area originally known as the City of Lafayette. The area is now

Prytania Street is one of the few homes occasionally open for public tours. It was built in 1858 in the Greek Revival style and has a distinctive octagonal turret, added in the late 19th century.

House, on Prytania Street, dates back to the 1830s and is surrounded by a large plantation-like garden enclosed in a copy of the original white picket fence. Thomas Toby was a Philadelphia businessman who built the simple Greek Revival structure well above the swampy ground to protect it from flooding. This area of the Garden District is thought to be the oldest.

Colonel Short's Villa, at the corner of Prytania and Fourth, is known for its unusual cast-iron cornstalk fence. It is said that Colonel Short had the fence, with its morning glories intertwined with corn stalks, built because his wife was homesick for her native Kentucky.

The Women's Guild of the New Orleans Opera Association House on

Bourbon Street

THE French Quarter is a six-by-twelve-block area along the crescent bank of the Mississippi River which stretches from the river to North Rampart Street between Canal Street and Esplanade Avenue. Also known as the Vieux Carre' (Old Square), the area was first settled by the French under Jean Baptiste le Moyne, Sieur de Bienville in 1718. He chose a spot that had long served as a portage for Indians between the Mississippi and Lake Pontchartrain. He named the settlement La Nouvelle Orleans, in honor of the regent of France, Philippe, Duke of Orleans. The original settlement was designed to guard the southern opening to France's empire in the New World. The city was laid out around the Place de'Armes, now Jackson Square. The first residents included French convicts, German indentured servants and Black and Native American slaves.

In its earliest years, New Orleans was a supply base for the thousands of European settlers lured to Louisiana by the promise of an easy life. Furs, lumber, cotton, sugar and rice were traded for manufactured goods from Europe and for slaves from the West Indies. A society of wealthy slave-owning planters and merchants developed in and around the growing city.

The French Quarter is where Creoles, proud descendants of the original French and Spanish settlers, built their city of charming town houses, a cathedral, market center and entertainment theaters. Theirs was a genteel and sophisticated society - until the influx of Anglo-Saxon Americans following the Louisiana Purchase in 1803.

The coming of the Civil War in the 1860's ended the French Quarter's Golden Era and it fell into disrepair until fifty years ago when the buildings were slowly restored to their former splendor. The French Quarter not only regained its place in the heart of the city but became world famous for Bourbon Street, home of New Orleans jazz and exciting night life to rival that found anywhere in the world.

Bourbon Street

THE French Quarter today is a fascinating combination of residences, shops, restaurants and offices. It is an active part of this port city, offering entertainment and dining day and night. Most of the area, with the notable exception of Bourbon Street, is strictly regulated to maintain its authenticity and style.

Lower Bourbon Street, with its flashy neon lights, varied entertainment menu and late-night attractions, offers an interesting counterpoint to the historically accurate and carefully restored buildings of the late 1700's to mid-1800's. This area of Bourbon Street and the French Quarter has come to symbolize New Orleans' jazz-loving, night-life rich side. Here, the city's motto "Let the good times roll" aptly describes the many nightclubs and bars along this world famous thoroughfare. Dixieland jazz swings from the clubs and from street musicians day and

night. Such clubs as Bayard's and the Famous Door invite you to listen to Dixieland and Creole jazz while enjoying one of their unusual house specialty drinks. Lulu White Mahogany Hall was established in 1897 and has moved to the site of the first Bourbon Street jazz nightclub. The hall maintains its turn-of-the-century style.

The French Quarter is known not only for its night life and jazz. It's equally famous for its Creole cuisine. Dishes, hot and spicy or rich and flavorful, are offered at establishments ranging from tiny street carts to full service restaurants. There's a treat for every taste, a meal for any appetite, large or small.

Shopping is another delight in the French Quarter. A large selection of shops offers everything from the latest fashions to fine arts and tourist trinkets.

Balconies

MANY of the French Quarter's European-style buildings are ornamented with intricate lacy wrought iron balconies, fences and gates. The delicate detailing of this work adds a light, airy touch to the buildings.

Until 1930, wrought iron was produced almost entirely by hand in "puddling" furnaces where molten pig iron was stirred with a long-handled tool called a "rabble" until the metal was purified. It was then squeezed into sections

known as "blooms" which were hand-rolled and hand-formed into a variety of intricate patterns. The modern method of casting iron creates similar, but less intricate, decorations. In most instances, purified iron is poured into forms and allowed to cool without hand decoration.

The building at Royal and St. Peter streets, as well as many of the buildings in the French Quarter, have preserved fine examples of both wrought iron and cast iron balconies. Many

unique designs may be seen on balconies adorning the second and third story apartments and town homes of the area.

Rue Royale is often called the street of balconies for its many fine examples of craftsmanship. The Labranche House, 700 Royale, built in the 1830's, is the most photographed corner in the city.

Residents of New Orleans take advantage of the almost tropical climate of the city to create living works of art on their balconies. With little or no snow and only an occasional freeze, New Orleans is a sea of constant changing color. Each season brings a new variety of blossom to brighten the balconies throughout the city.

During the Civil War, these flower-draped balconies served a different purpose. From them, hidden by plants and ironwork, the ladies of New Orleans threw pots, pans and insults at the passing Federal soldiers who invaded their city. Incensed, General Butler issued the Woman Order in 1862, threatening to treat these ladies as women of the street and prosecute them as such. Several brave but unfortunate women endured just such a fate before the war ended.

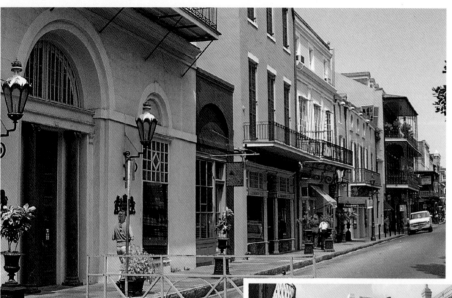

Most of the buildings in the French Quarter are built of cypress timbers, chinked with clay bricks, and plastered over for protection from the weather. The roofs are usually flat tiles. Many of the buildings served a dual purpose. The first floor was reserved for a shop or business office, the second for family living. The third floor would be either slave quarters or the family's sleeping rooms. If the third floor was used by the family, the servants were usually housed in a separate building which usually included the kitchen. This not only kept the slaves separate from their masters, but allowed the hot cooking to be done far away from the main house.

Most homes had balconies adorned with intricate wrought iron railings where residents could sit and catch a cool breeze and watch the goings-on along the street, surely as entertaining as today's television. Access to the balconies was through tall, shuttered windows which could be left open to allow the river's cooling breezes to "air condition" the homes.

MANY of the buildings in the French Quarter date back to the early 1800's and have been carefully restored. The Old Absinthe House at 238 Rue Bourbon is a Vieux Carre' landmark. It was built in 1806 by Pedro Front and the Francisco Juncadella of Barcelona, Spain. Still owned by the original family, the building once served as the headquarters of Jeane Lafitte, "the patriotic pirate." After more than 250 years, the restaurant and drinking establishment in the building caters to visitors from all over the world - many of whom have added their business cards and addresses to the collection on the walls.

Brennan's Restaurant on Rue Royale was built in 1801 as a combination home and business. In 1804, it was the home of the Louisiana Bank. It was also the boyhood home of famed chess player, Paul Morphy. Today, Brennan's presents mouthwatering Creole cuisine from the original building.

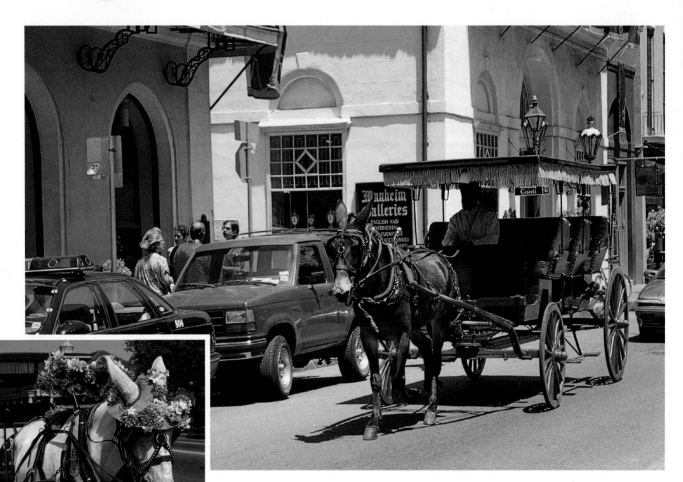

MULE-DRAWN carriages await passengers from morning until late in the evening at stands on Jackson Square at Decatur Street in the heart of the French Quarter. The placid mules replaced horses years ago when they proved to be more tolerant of New Orleans' heat and humidity. These large beasts, a cross between a horse and a donkey, pace gracefully through the city's streets, pulling carriages and surreys filled with delighted tourists. Getting in the spirit of New Orleans style fun, they often wear outlandish flowered hats while maintaining their dignity, unruffled by traffic, noise and pedestrians. Knowledgeable carriage drivers act as guides, pointing out the sights and explaining the history and folklore of the area.

Bourbon Street is the only street in New Orleans that allows neon signs, and full advantage of that fact is taken. It's also a street where you can get your fill of girlie shows, strip tease dancers, female impersonators, old-time burlesque and even French can-can.

Of course, Bourbon Street, the "Playground of the South," is famous for its Dixieland jazz as well. As night descends upon the street, rollicking music can be heard coming from club after club and you can choose from honky tonk piano to bluesy sax and "licorice stick" clarinet.

There's no finer place for traditional New Orleans jazz than Preservation Hall. This establishment is for the purist whose ears crave the sweet sounds of old-time New Orleans jazz.

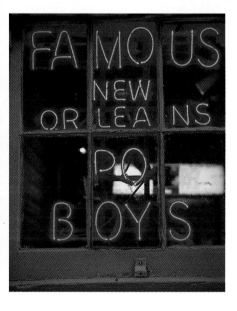

If you want to party down, or just wet your whistle, there's no livelier place than Pat O'Brien's Bar, next door to Preservation Hall. It's the party animal's heaven and its "hurricane" is famous.

For seafood and Southern specialties, you can take your choice from street vendors to eateries with an all-you-can-eat philosophy where the succulent crab or shrimp just keeps coming.

Decatur Street

THE Cafe du Monde on Decatur Street marks the beginning of the famous French Market. The cafe has been a landmark in the city for generations. Natives and guests alike make their way to this wonderful eatery for cafe' au lait, a mixture of equal parts strong chicory-laced coffee and hot milk.

Nothing makes a better accompaniment for this famous coffee beverage than beignets (pronounced ben-yays), which are square French doughnuts deep fried and then dipped in powdered sugar.

Lucky guests are allowed to peek into the kitchen where they can watch this French delicacy rolled, cut and dropped into hot oil to fry until golden, crispy brown.

Tujague's, also on Decatur Street, was established in 1856 and is the sec-

ond oldest restaurant in the city. Once called Madame Begues, Tujague's is revered for its six course table d'Hote and the oldest standing bar in the city.

The huge old warehouse building that once housed the Jackson or JAX Brewery at Jackson Square and the river, has been converted into a three-section shopping and entertainment

complex. Shops, galleries, restaurants and bars fill the inside, often jammin' with live music. The third floor is devoted to Louisiana's Living Treasures, a work, display and performance area for local artists, crafts persons and musicians.

The Louisiana General store offers visitors the opportunity to take some genuine New Orleans' culinary skills home through its morning cooking classes.

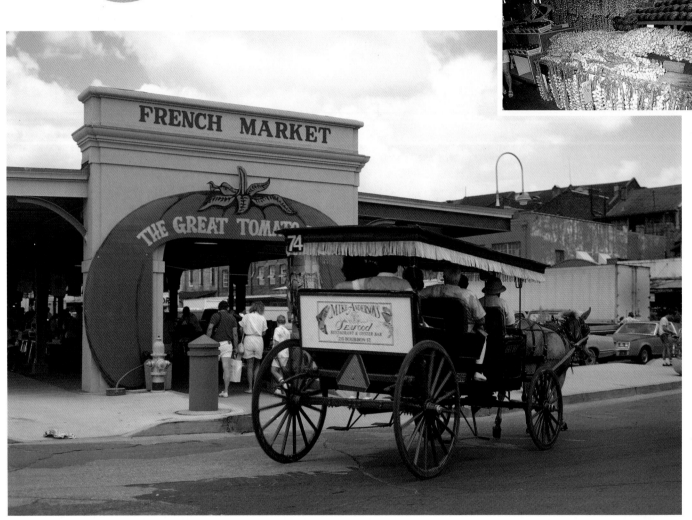

French Market

Long before New Orleans became the bustling city it is today, Choctaw Indians gathered where the French Market now stands to trade with other tribes and the White men who were settling in the region. Soon German traders joined the Indians in the bustling open-air market on Decatur Street at St. Ann Street, and busy trade with the French and Spanish settlers ensued.

In 1791, the city built buildings for the traders. In 1812, a hurricane destroyed the market but it was soon rebuilt. Few of those original buildings still stand but one, built in 1822, remains. Most of the remaining structures were built in the 1930's. Many today are glass-enclosed.

Visitors to this colorful cornucopia will be dazzled by the variety and beauty of the fresh Louisiana produce which is sold. Vendors arrange their wares in colorful patterns resembling delightful abstract paintings awash in primary colors. On most weekends, talented street performers and musicians practice their lively crafts throughout the market.

Jackson Square

THE city of New Orleans was laid out in the French style on an elevated piece of land in the sweeping curve of the Mississippi River. The streets branch out from a central square, the Place d'Armes. Today, that same square, renamed Jackson Square, is at the heart of the French Quarter. The square is lined with the St. Louis Cathedral, the Colonial Cabildo and Presbytere, the Pontalba Apartments and the Mississippi River.

Jackson Square

ORIGINALLY called Place d'Armes and designed as a military parade square, Jackson Square was the center of the new city of New Orleans.

Place d'Armes was renamed Jackson Square in 1849 for General Andrew Jackson, hero of the Battle of New Orleans in the War of 1812, and later the seventh president of the United States. The equestrian statue of Jackson was erected in 1856. The words carved on the base, "The Union must and shall be preserved," were placed there in honor of the Federal troops who occupied the city during the Civil War.

The beauty of the square today belays its fascinating and sometimes macabre history. It was the site of the signing of the Louisiana Purchase, making New Orleans officially part of the expanding United States. It was also the site of public executions - sometimes by such gruesome means as hanging, rending limb from limb and burning at the stake.

One side of the square is located on the Mississippi River. The lovely edifice of the St. Louis Cathedral, built in 1794, graces the far side. The cathedral is flanked by the Presbytere, begun in 1795 and completed in 1847, and the Cabildo, built in 1799.

The two remaining sides of the square are lined with the Pontalba Apartments, built in the late 1840's, and the oldest apartment buildings in the United States.

The square is landscaped in a sun pattern with pedestrian walkways radiating from the statue in the center. This style of garden design became popular in the royal court of King Louis XIV, the Sun King.

Street artists display their paintings along the park's fences and many will draw the portraits of

passersby for a nominal charge. Most are also very knowledgeable about the city and provide much local insight and color.

Residents and visitors alike gather in the square to watch the artists, sample the wares of vendors, listen to street musicians or just enjoy the beauty of a New Orleans day.

Saint Louis Cathedral

SAINT LOUIS Cathedral is the oldest active cathedral in the United States. The building was built in 1794 to replace two others which had burned. It was remodeled and enlarged in 1850. In 1964, the cathedral was elevated to the status of minor basilica, one of only 15 in this country.

In 1987, Pope John Paul II held a prayer service for clergy at the cathedral. In his honor, the pedestrian mall in front was renamed Place Jean Paul Deux.

The cathedral is open to worshippers and visitors alike and free tours are conducted

daily. The arched two-story ceiling adds an elegant and open feeling to the two-story chapel. Flag holders on the second floor balcony hold the flags representing the nations of the world.

The rectory behind the cathedral houses a fascinating collection of the church's records and chronicles marriages, baptisms and deaths dating from as far back as 1731.

Flanking the St. Louis Cathedral are two nearly identical Spanish Colonial-style buildings, the Presbytere and the Cabildo. The Presbytere was begun in 1795 but not completed until 1847. It was to have been the priest's house but served instead as a Spanish, and later, American, courthouse.

The Cabildo was built in 1799 for the Spanish Council, or Cabildo, and replaced a building demolished by fire. A devastating fire in 1988 destroyed the top floor of the building, but most of the antiquities were

rescued. The building served the Spanish Cabildo, the territorial government of France and the Confederacy. Today, both buildings are part of the Louisiana State Museum.

Pontalba Apartments

THE Pontalba Apartments are two sets of European-style row house apartment buildings, one on each side of Jackson Square. They were built in the late 1840's by Baroness Micaela Pontalba, daughter of a wealthy Spaniard, and are the oldest apartment buildings in the United States.

1850's House has been restored to resemble one of the apartments as it looked in the 1850's. The first floor was to be used as a shop and kitchen. The second floor served as living quarters and the third floor was devoted to bedrooms. The fourth floor contained the servants' quarters. All the furnishings, accessories, utensils and toys are from the 1850s. The house is maintained by, and tours are offered through, the Louisiana State Museum.

The baroness is credited with helping fund the landscaping in Jackson Park and the construction of the Jackson statue. She is also credited with the introduction of cast or molded iron work which eventually replaced much of the old hand wrought work of the French Quarter. The baroness' initials may still be seen worked into the design on the ironwork of the buildings.

Homes & Courtyards

UNLIKE most cities where alleyways are dark, dank and dangerous, the passages between buildings in the French Quarter of New Orleans are often works of art in themselves. Many lead to delightful, secluded courtyards behind private homes. Others are open to the public. A number of the restaurants have lovely courtyards where patrons may enjoy a fine repast under the shade of bright umbrellas or graceful trees, surrounded by lush flowering plants, sculpture and ornate wrought iron.

One of New Orleans' most beautiful courtyards can be found at The Court of Two Sisters Restaurant on Royal Street. The restaurant building itself dates back to 1832. The restaurant is named for two sisters who long ago ran a dry goods shop in the building. If you're lucky, you might be allowed to stroll down the carriageway for a view of the private courtyard.

The Beauregard-Keyes House on Charles Street also has a large and lovely courtyard in the rear. At its back is the studio of novelist Frances Parkinson Keyes. A prolific writer, Keyes wrote 40 novels in the studio, all in longhand. Viewing the courtyard, it is easy to see where some of her inspiration must have come from.

The property also has a wonderful walled garden which extends to the corner of Chartres and Ursulines streets. The garden, in bloom all

during the year, is laid out in the same sun pattern as Jackson Square and has been used several times as a romantic setting in movies filmed in the area.

The home itself was the temporary residence of Confederate General P.G.T. Beauregard. Keyes was responsible for restoring the stately 19th century mansion to its former glory.

Flowering plants, glittering fountains, curious statuary and elegant brick flooring enhance many of the courtyards or 'courts' in the French Quarter. It is not unusual to see an artist attempting to capture the serenity and beauty of one of these havens on canvas.

Homes & Courtyards

NEW ORLEANS is a city of lacy wrought iron balconies and fences. Classic examples of each may be seen throughout the French Quarter and Garden District. Many of the intricate hand-wrought and cast iron fences in the French Quarter lightly conceal, yet offer enticing views of, charming courtyards beyond.

A most unusual example of cast iron fence is the Corn Stalk Fence at 915 Rue Royale. The fence is believed to have been erected in 1830 at the height of cast iron fence's popularity in the city. The fence is painted in natural colors and pumpkins form the bases of the poles.

Many of the houses in the French Quarter have been carefully preserved, although some were lost before serious preservation efforts took place. Some still function as private homes while others have been turned into museums, hotels, restaurants and bed and breakfast establishments. While all are not

historically accurate in their restoration and uses, they do provide a unique opportunity to experience New Orleans as it was in the early 19th century.

While on Royal Street, a visit to the Gallier House will offer insights into elegant French Quarter living in the mid-19th century. The home was built by noted architect James Gallier Jr. in 1857 and has been completely restored, including the servants' quarters and grounds. There is even a carriageway complete with carriage, the only one in the city. Educational films are presented on early architectural styles and 19th century living.

The house at 915 Rue Royale, with its whimsical corn stalk fence, has been turned into a charming hotel, maintaining its true New Orleans style.

Many of the residences in the French Quarter have lovely courtyards beside or behind them. Some, like the one here, feature brickwork and refreshing little fountains.

Pat O'Briens

No visit to New Orleans can be considered complete without a stop at Pat O'Brien's Bar on the corner of world-famous Bourbon Street and St. Peter Street. The daring insist on sampling the famous Pat O'Brien's Hurricane, a deceptively sweet but highly potent drink served in a tall lantern-shaped souvenir glass. Drinks are served in front of or inside the pub/restaurant or on the beautiful courtyard, all accompanied by cheery jazz piano music.

Bourbon Street is a partier's mecca today but it wasn't always that way. Until World War II, this was a quiet residential neighborhood complete with small shops and an elegant opera house. The opera house burned in 1919, never to be replaced. The sounds emanating from Bourbon Street today include jazz, blues and modern rock.

New Orleans has its fair share of folk tales and Bourbon Street is no exception. Lafitte's Blacksmith Shop, a picturesque saloon in one of the oldest buildings in the city, is purported to not only have been a blacksmith shop but actually a front for pirate Jean Lafitte and his crew. The building was constructed in 1772 and is one of only a few surviving examples of soft brick reinforced with timbers, a method of construction much favored by early settlers in the region.

Preservation Hall

For the traditional jazz lover, step next door from Pat O'Brien's Bar to Preservation Hall where old-time New Orleans jazz is performed by the finest native singers and musicians in the country.

This small building may look a bit seedy on the outside, but is a cultural landmark de-

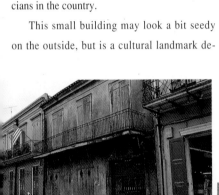

voutly enshrining the jazz traditions of the 1920's. No food or drink is served in this serious, no-frills music emporium. Guests pay an admission fee and are welcome to sit through as many sets as they like. A rotating calendar of some of jazz music's legends and soon-to-

be legends keep true music lovers glued to their seats for set after set.

The atmosphere may be understated, the sign above the door is printed on a couple of old instrument cases, but make no mistake, this is New Orleans' most famous jazz club.

Jazz and Mardi Gras are two of the things New Orleans is most famous for - and rightly so.

The term Mardi Gras has come to denote the whole celebration of what is actually Carnival. Mardi Gras is the culmination of anywhere from several weeks to more than a month of festivities leading up to Ash Wednesday and the beginning of Lent. Mardi Gras itself is a 24-hour celebration held each year on Fat Tuesday, which falls in February or early March, the day before Ash Wednesday.

There are no clear records regarding how Carnival actually got its start in Europe. Some believe it an offshoot of pagan religious holidays. Others think the custom began in the Middle Ages. In Renaissance times, Rome is known to have held huge feasts before the beginning of the long deprivation of Lent.

France is one of the countries which celebrated Mardi Gras early in its history, so it is no surprise that when French-Canadian explorer Pierre La Myne, Sieur d'Iberville, came to what is now New Orleans on March 3, Mardi Gras Day in 1699, he named it Pointe du Mardi Gras.

America borrowed the tradition of Mardi Gras first in Mobile, Alabama, followed by New Orleans in the 1820's. Oddly, American settlers, not the French or Spanish, were the first to establish the parades traditional of the festival. In the beginning, bands of masked revelers marched through the streets of the city throwing confetti and flour into the faces of onlookers on Mardi Gras day. These early celebrants were more intent on mischief and drink than celebration.

The early Creole aristocracy chose to celebrate the coming of Lent in a more refined way by hosting private gala balls. Additionally, "Quadroon" balls were held where wealthy planters escorted their "free women of color." Quadroons were the descendants of slaves and White planters. These women were often chosen by wealthy planters as mistresses. They were kept in town houses and considered almost, but not quite, the equal of the planter's White wife.

On February 24, 1857, a group of approximately 60 men calling themselves Mastick Krewe of Comus, after the god of revelry, created the forerunner of today's Mardi Gras celebrations. Dressed as demons, they paraded the streets of New Orleans with two floats

and a torchlight brigade. The group was made up of Creoles from the French Quarter and wealthy Americans, or Saxons, from the other side of Canal Street. Created as a secret men's society, they also held a ball for 3,000 people at the Gaiety Theater and a tradition that continues today was born.

It didn't take long for this city that loves to party to catch Mardi Gras fever. Mechanized floats were added in 1839 and that was only the beginning.

I N 1872, a group of businessmen organized the Krewe of Rex (Latin for king) and hosted a daytime parade for the visit of His Imperial Highness, the Grand Duke Alexis of Russia. They chose the Carnival colors still used today - gold for power, purple for justice and green for faith.

Prompted by the success of other krewes, new organizations formed, several choosing to introduce their young daughters to society at debutante teas and balls during Carnival. Young ladies of the finest families were presented to society at "white gown balls."

In 1969, a group of businessmen formed Bacchus, named for the god of wine. Their first parade contained floats that dwarfed the Rex parade, and the king was Danny Kaye. The gala was held in the Rivergate Convention Center and open to all.

In 1974, Endymion topped that with a party for more than 10,000, aptly called the Extravaganza, which is now held in the Louisiana Superdome.

Today, parade after parade of elaborate multi-storied floats, fabulously costumed participants and entertaining musical groups wend

their way down the city's streets during the week-long extravaganza.

The celebration of Carnival officially begins the week of January 6 with a debutante ball called Twelfth Night. Carnival events build until the week before Fat Tuesday. There are balls and parades including those of the Knights of Babylon, Momus, the Krewe of Hermes, Endymion and Bacchus.

Mardi Gras Tuesday is the climax of the Carnival season, complete with King Rex and his parade. A special treat is watching the Mardi

Gras Indians, a group of Black men in fantastic feathered costumes who tour the French Quarter.

The Rex Ball, held at Municipal Auditorium, closes out the celebration of Carnival and Mardi Gras when the king and queen cross to the other side of the auditorium to join the Mastick Krewe of Comus king and queen at their ball. The couples exchange partners and sit side by side on thrones to mark the close of the evening and of Mardi Gras.

Although the Carnival and Mardi Gras tradition are borrowed, nowhere in the world do folks have as much fun and pageantry as each late winter in New Orleans.

Every spring, New Orleans pays homage to jazz with its annual Jazz and Heritage Festival. The infield of the Fair Grounds Race Track comes alive with music to suit any taste including: contemporary jazz, rhythm and blues, Gospel, pop, Afro-Caribbean, Cajun, blues, zydeco, ragtime, folk, Latin, Rock, country and western and Bluegrass, all

performed on 12 stages and an indoor performance area in the grandstand.

Fairgoers can also sample over 90 varieties of Louisiana foods from muffeletta to alligator and red beans and rice, while being entertained by passing marching brass bands.

A crafts fair features hundreds of handicrafts and fine arts, some offering hands on exhibits. In Congo Square, now called Beauregard Square, an area which honors the cultural heritage of African-Americans, traditional African crafts and performances can be found.

No one exemplifies New Orleans jazz like Louis - Satchmo - Armstrong, possibly the father of American jazz. A

tradition thought to have originated in the 1890's with Black Creoles, stars like Armstrong, Jelly Roll Morton and Sidney Bechet, gave the music voice, complete with lyrical flourishes and low down blues notes blending to form a unique combination.

Armstrong's life was a rags-to-riches tale. Born August 4, 1901, he grew up in a New Orleans ghetto, traveled the Missis-

sippi River playing on riverboats and eventually played in the finest clubs the world over. Louis Armstrong Park, on North Rampart Street, honors the jazzman with a statue and fountain. Sadly, Armstrong was never welcome to play in the fanciest clubs in his home town.

New Orleans cooking is a melting pot of culinary styles influenced by African, Spanish, French, Choctaw Indian and Acadian immigrants. African slaves introduced gumbo, the African word for okra. This vegetable was used as a thickening agent in dishes like the more modern gumbo. The Spanish added tomatoes and peppers, used in jambalaya, a variation on Spanish paella. Choctaw Indians added sassafras as a thickening agent, and corn, creating grits and macque-choux, an Acadian dish consisting of corn, bell peppers and onion. The Acadians, exiled from Nova Scotia, introduced inexpensive meats, seasonal game, fish and simple garden produce to the menu, rounding out a true New Orleans Gumbo.

Much Cajun cooking is based on the "Holy Trinity," onion, bell pepper and celery. Combined with rice, filé, red pepper, Tabasco sauce and a hen, all thickened with roux, a flour-based thickener, the Holy Trinity creates a dish fit for any Cajun household.

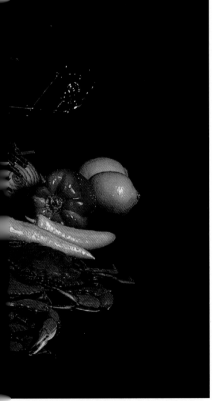

Oysters Bienville

2	Tbsp butter
¼	cup finely chopped shallots
¼	cup chopped parsley
2	Tbsp flour
1	cup warm cream
1	cup liquid (milk, oyster liquor or chicken stock)
½	cup broken pieces of shrimp
½	cup mushroom pieces
2	egg yolks
⅓	cup Chablis wine
	black or cayenne pepper
2	dozen oysters
½	cup seasoned bread crumbs
4	Tbsp parmesan cheese
	paprika
	lemon wedges

Sauté shallots (green onions) and parsley in a heavy pan until soft. Add flour and blend. The sauce is usually kept white, but the old Creole way was to allow it to brown lightly. Add cream slowly, keeping heat low and blending well. Add remaining liquid gradually. Beat the egg yolks into the Chablis, add shrimp and mushrooms and stir into sauce. Seasoning may be added into the wine and egg mixture. Continue to cook until well thickened (sauce may be made a day ahead). Place oysters on half shells (or in a casserole on a layer of bread crumbs) and ladle sauce over them. Sprinkle with a topping of bread crumbs and cheese (optional), and dust with paprika. Shells are usually baked in a shallow pan of rock salt which has been preheated in a 400 degree oven for one half hour. Return to 400 degree oven for 15 minutes until golden brown. Serve with lemon wedges.

Red Beans and Rice

1 ham bone
½ lb ham, cubed
1 lb dried red beans
1 large onion, chopped
1 cup chopped green onions, tops
   and bottoms
¼ cup chopped bell pepper
¼ cup chopped parsley
½ tsp basil
2 bay leaves
¼ cup butter
   salt and cayenne pepper to taste

Kidney beans will do, but small dark red beans are better. Put them in a heavy pot with enough water to cover, bring to a rolling boil for a couple of minutes, then soak overnight in that same water. In the morning, bring to a boil again and add all other ingredients. Reduce heat and simmer for at least 3 hours. The ham bone is important for flavor. Be sure beans are not old. They should become very creamy, but most will remain whole. Add cold water as needed. Goes well with smoked sausage and sliced raw onions.

Serve over fluffy long grain rice cooked as follows: Bring 3 quarts of water to a rapid boil. Add salt, one tablespoon of oil and one of vinegar, and one cup of rice. Oil will keep water from boiling over and vinegar will let each grain fall to itself. Reduce heat and sim-

mer exactly 18 minutes. Drain in a colander, rinse off excess starch with cold water and steam in colander until well warmed again.

Mardi Gras Salad

Wash one head of lettuce well, dry, and tear into pieces. Slice one yellow bell pepper into long narrow strips. Wash ⅛ of a head of purple cabbage, drain well, and slice into long thin pieces.

Mix a Creole Mustard Salad Dressing by blending ⅓ cup Creole Mustard (a dark mustard), ¼ cup red wine or sherry vinegar, one small onion, peeled and quartered, and salt and pepper to taste in a blender. Slowly pour in oil while blending. Arrange salad with lettuce in the bottom of the bowl and purple cabbage and yellow bell pepper strips scattered over the top. Pour dressing over the salad.

Recipe from Cookin' Cajun Cooking School in New Orleans.

Shrimp Creole

¼	cup flour
¼	cup bacon grease
1½	cups chopped onions
1	cup chopped green onions
1	cup chopped celery with leaves
1	cup chopped bell pepper
2	cloves garlic, minced
1	six-ounce can tomato paste
1	16 ounce can chopped tomatoes with liquid
1	8 ounce can tomato sauce
1	cup water
5	teaspoons salt
1	teaspoon pepper
½	teaspoon red pepper (optional)
	Tabasco sauce to taste
2-3	bay leaves
1	teaspoon sugar
1	teaspoon Worcestershire sauce
1	tablespoon lemon juice
4	pounds peeled raw shrimp
½	cup chopped parsley
2-3	cups cooked rice

Make a dark brown roux of flour and bacon grease in a large heavy pot. Add onions, green onions, celery, bell pepper and garlic and saute until soft. Add tomato paste and mix this well with vegetables. Add all other ingredients except last three. Simmer slowly for one hour, covered, stirring occasionally. Add shrimp and cook until done, 5 to 15 minutes. This should set awhile and is much better made the day before and reheated but not boiled. Freezes well. Add parsley just before serving. Serve over rice. Serves 10.

Seafood Gumbo

½	cup flour
½	cup vegetable oil
1	large onion
1	pod garlic
½	bell pepper, chopped
¼	cup chopped parsley
2	lbs shrimp
1	lb crabmeat
1	quart oysters with oyster water
2	bay leaves
1	Tbsp Worcestershire sauce
2	quarts or more of water
	salt, pepper and tabasco and filé to taste

Make a roux by browning ½ cup flour and ½ cup of well heated vegetable oil. Lower heat and add water gradually. Add onion, garlic, pepper and parsley and cook 30 minutes. Add crabmeat. This can be freshly cleaned crabs or fresh or frozen lump crabmeat, but it is nice to have the crab claws and a few chunks from the body of the crab in the gumbo.

At this time, add the bay leaves, Worcestershire sauce and seasonings, but save filé. Cook 15 minutes. Add the shrimp and oysters and cook about 5 more minutes on a high heat until oysters begin to curl. Do not overcook shrimp and oysters. Cut the heat off, add filé and serve. Filé is powdered sassafras leaves and is a thickener, so do not overdo it. A tablespoonful is about right. If you cannot fine filé, add thinly sliced young tender okra at the beginning for thickening.

Among those buried in St. Louis Cemetery #1 are Etienne Bore', father of the sugar industry, Homer Plessy of Plessy vs. Ferguson fame which established the separate-but-equal Jim Crow laws for Blacks and Whites in the South in 1892 and - Marie Laveau, queen of voodoo (pictured left).

Laveau is one of the most famous, or infamous, people interred in the Basin Street cemetery. Marie practiced her craft of creating voodoo dolls, hexes and charms in the 1820's and had a large fol-

Nოt many cities consider their burial grounds to be tourist attractions, but New Orleans does. In fact, they have a group called Save our Cemeteries which offers guided walking tours of St. Louis Cemetery #1 and the Lafayette Cemetery #1 in the Garden District.

St. Louis Cemetery #1, the oldest cemetery in the city, is typical of the unique above ground burial practices initiated by the French and Spanish. With its notoriously soggy ground and frequent floods, the dead could not expect to stay buried. They would have floated to the surface, an annoying habit at best. Instead, the French and Spanish placed their dead in ornate masonry above-ground vaults and tombs. Although modern methods allow underground burial these days, many New Orleans families still opt for the old method.

lowing among the African slaves. She and her followers met in Congo Square (now called Beauregard Square), amid the talking drums, to dance, worship and speak their native tongue.

Marie Laveau's daughter, another Marie, carried on her mother's traditions and her orgies are legendary. She is buried at St. Louis Cemetery #2, four blocks from her mother, on Clairborne Avenue. Both graves are still marked with fresh chalked X's by those who believe in the women's supernatural powers. The New Orleans Historic Voodoo Museum provides guided walking tours of these cemeteries.

The white-walled Lafayette Cemetery takes up the 1600 block of Washington Avenue in the Garden District. It resides in what used to be the city of Jefferson in the early 1800's, the location Americans or "Kaintucks" settled after the Louisiana Purchase. Interred here are the families who built the surrounding mansions. This cemetery gained fame in Anne Rice's trilogy, Vampire Chronicles.

Metairie Cemetery on Metairie Road has many lavish examples of above-ground tombs, and it is possible to drive through the park to examine them.

Audubon Park is located on what was once the plantation of Etienne de Bore', founder of the granulated sugar industry in Louisiana. The 1884-85 World's Industrial and Cotton Centennial Exposition was held on this site. None of the original buildings of the plantation or exposition remain. The current park was designed by internationally known landscape architect Frederick Law Olmstead and includes the zoo, a golf course, wading and swimming pools, a riding stable, picnic and play areas, tennis courts and winding pathways for bikes, hikers and joggers. The park and zoo are named for John James Audubon, the famous naturalist and painter, who spent years working in and around New Orleans. A statue in the park honors him.

AUDUBON ZOO, in the 340 acre Audubon Park on Charles Avenue, is one of the finest zoos in the country. It was completely revamped in the late 1970's. Following the natural habitat concept of display and breeding, the zoo features realistic exhibits of the Louisiana Swamp, Tropical Bird House, flamingo pond, big cats and sea lions.

AQUARIUM OF THE AMERICAS is located in Woldenberg Riverfront Park at the Mississippi River end of Canal Street. The modern aquarium uses 60 separate displays ranging from 500 to 500,000 gallons of captive water to exhibit more than 7,000 different aquatic creatures.

There are four major areas of the aquarium. They include the Amazon River Basin, Caribbean Reef, Mississippi River and Gulf Coast. Each is a separate, self contained, realistic environment designed so that viewers actually feel a part of the watery world they view. During the day, divers may be seen in the Caribbean Reef display feeding and playing with the aquatic creatures who dwell there.

A well-landscaped park surrounds the aquarium and offers a charming place for a quiet stroll with a magnificent view of Mississippi River activity.

Quarter, it boasts an exotic and enticing array of shops and restaurants.

In front of the Spanish Plaza entrance to Riverwalk is a statue of Bernardo de Galvez, Spanish Governor of Louisiana in the 1780's.

A sparkling fountain plays a musical tune outside another entrance to the shopping mecca.

Once the site of the 1984 World's Fair, the shopping area is connected to a

Dᴏᴡɴ several steps from Spanish Plaza outside the St. Louis Cathedral, where Canal Street meets the river, an old riverfront warehouse district has been transformed into a half-mile long shopping and entertainment mecca called Riverwalk Marketplace. Said to resemble a futuristic, indoor version of the French

promenade along the Mississippi River's edge. Plaques along the walkway recall the history and folklore of the area and the river. The city's streetcars run to and from the Riverwalk Marketplace throughout the day and evening.

The New Orleans Convention Center, built for the World's Fair, has been expanded to 700,000 square feet. One of the largest such facilities in the world, it is booked a decade into the future.

The city of New Orleans operates the historic St. Charles Avenue and Riverfront streetcar lines. Established in 1835, streetcars were the main mode of transportation in the city for many years. Now, commuters, sightseers and shoppers along the two routes use modern reproductions of the original cars to get about this fascinating city.

One route of the charming vehicles is along picturesque St. Charles Avenue.

The Riverfront streetcar runs just short of two miles along the Mississippi from the French Quarter to the Convention Center. One of the city's most famous vehicles, A Streetcar Named Desire, immortalized by Tennessee Williams, is enshrined on Barracks Street.

THE riverfront is and always has been a vital part of New Orleans lifestyle and is one of the fastest growing and most exciting areas of the city today.

Although the Mississippi River has long been valued for its commercial uses, New Orleans honors it in many other ways as well. The Crescent City was founded on the river to provide protection for French territory in the Mississippi Valley and to facilitate transportation of troops and supplies from the sea.

Built on filled-in marshlands, the city is protected from flooding by levees, drainage canals and pumping stations. The Bonnet Carre' Spillway 40 miles upstream can be opened to divert floodwater racing toward the city.

Over time, the city has spread out along the river for many miles. Its gridiron street patterns bending to accommodate the river's curving shoreline. Receiving directions from New Orleans residents is often interesting. The city is divided into Uptown, Downtown, Lakeside and Riverside. Uptown denotes the side of Canal Street where the Garden District

is located. Downtown includes the French Quarter and central city. Riverside denotes the area where the Garden District ends. Lakeside refers to anything toward Lake Pontchartrain. Uptown is also the University District, if you're not confused enough. Oh, and a banquette is a sidewalk, and natives call their city something that sounds more like "N'Awlins" than New Orleans.

There is a series of lovely parks located along the Mississippi River. Moonwalk, a park renovated during the term of Mayor "Moon" Landrieu, offers spectacular overviews of the city and the great Mississippi River. Woldenberg Riverfront Park, once the home of the 1984 World's Fair, hosts outdoor concerts in a setting sweetened by magnolia and crepe myrtle trees.

A not-to-be-missed cruise on one of the paddlewheelers plying the river offers a provocative perspective on a city which combines towering skyscrapers with wisteria-draped, wrought iron decorated buildings dating from the 1800's.

which makes a 45-mile cruise down the Mississippi and through the Intracoastal Waterway and Bayou Barataria/Lafitte area.

The Delta Queen Steamboat Company hosts overnight and lengthier cruises aboard the legendary Delta Queen and her sister ship, the Mississippi Queen.

New Orleans Paddlewheels, Inc. offers the Creole Queen and Cajun Queen for daily three-hour cruises downriver through the port of New Orleans and to the Chalmette Battlefield. Also available are five-hour tours of the bayous below

Nothing beats the romance of stepping back in time that can be had simply by boarding one of New Orleans' numerous riverboats for a cruise on the historic Mississippi River.

The New Orleans Steamboat Company floats a wide variety of cruises on their fleet of riverboats. Among the most interesting is the Natchez which leaves twice daily from the heart of the French Quarter and cruises the second busiest port in the world. The Natchez offers jazz dinner cruises as well as daytime trips. Another of the Company's steamboats is the Bayou Jean Lafitte

New Orleans and shorter harbor tours with meals and live jazz ensembles for entertainment. Both boats are authentic replicas of the steamers which plied these waters in the 1800's.

The President Riverboat offers weekend cruises with live dance bands and the Cotton Blossom travels from the Riverwalk shopping center to the Audubon Zoo. The Voyageur makes stops at the Chalmette Battlefield and then travels into bayou country by way of the Algiers Locks on a daily " River, Plantation and Bayou Cruise."

Then there's the Canal Street Ferry which will haul you and your car across the river for a tour of Algiers, where many of the Mardi Gras floats are constructed.

S HIPS from around the world share the harbor and piers of New Orleans with antique and reproduction paddlewheel steamboats. One of America's busiest waterways, the Mississippi welcomes ocean-going ships, tugboats with their improbably huge collection of barges and dredge boats busy keeping the channels clear.

Steam navigation opened the Mississippi Valley to shipping and New Or-

leans began to rival New York City as a leading United States port. The opening of the Erie Canal in 1825 and the laying of railroads from the Atlantic in the 1840's and 50's further increased the city's importance.

Before the Civil War, the city was the nation's greatest marketing center for slaves and cotton. In January 1861,

the state seceded from the Union. Being the main port for the Confederacy, New Orleans was soon attacked and overrun by Commander David Farragut. By May 1 of 1863, Union troops, under the command of General Benjamin Butler occupied the city.

After the war ended, New Orleans once again became a major river port and a large rail center. In the 1870's, the Mississippi below the city was deepened to a minimum depth of 26 feet, allowing access by large ocean-going vessels. In 1921, the Inner Harbor Navigation Canal, linking the Mississippi and Lake Pontchartrain, was completed.

The Jean Lafitte National Historical Park operates the Chalmette National Historic Park which preserves the battlefield where American forces, under the command of Andrew Jackson, turned back the British invasion of New Orleans in 1815. The Beauregard Plantation House, constructed in 1840 and the home of P.G.T. Beauregard, the Civil War general who opened fire on Fort Sumpter in Charleston Harbor, serves as a visitor's center.

The Greater New Orleans Bridge is an impressive twin span connecting New Orleans to the West Bank. The river below flows in a huge crescent-shaped arch around the city, 100 miles upstream of the Gulf of Mexico.

THE impressive Louisiana Superdome was built in 1975 at a cost of more than $180 million and is one of the largest buildings of its kind in the world. The building seats 100,000 people and can be partitioned off for small events like conventions, concerts and Mardi Gras balls. The building's roof covers nearly eight acres and there is a parking garage which accommodates 5,000 cars and 250 busses.

The Superdome's most important function is, of course, football. The New Orleans Saints football team calls the 27-story tall structure, with its 166,000-square-foot playing field, home. They play their home games here on Sundays. On Saturday afternoons,

Tulane University plays its home games on the same field. The famous LSU-Tulane battle is played here on odd-numbered years and Grambling and Southern universities face each other on the gridiron each November for the Bayou Classic. Every New Year's Day, the Superdome hosts the Sugar Bowl and, at four year intervals, the Super Bowl.

The Superdome isn't used only for football. Other sports get their day. The NCAA Final Four is held at the Superdome when it is played in New Orleans, and the Sugar Bowl Basketball Tournament is held annually the week preceding the football classic. Boxing events are also held here occasionally.

In addition to the sporting events, the Superdome schedules conventions, Mardi Gras balls, the circus and ice-skating shows. The National Republican Convention was held here in 1988, and several times a year it is filled to capacity with music lovers ready to be entertained by the world's hottest or most classic concerts.

Guided tours of this monolithic edifice are given when it is not in use. They include the ballrooms, private suites, the press box and main arena. Lunch is served in the Stadium Club.

The area surrounding the Superdome has developed into a modern complex of interconnected buildings which serve and compliment the Superdome. They include several hotels, the Texaco Building and Poydras Plaza. The New Orleans Centre, situated between the Superdome and the Hyatt Regency Hotel, is the city's newest and fanciest shopping mall and draws many conventioners and sports enthusiasts who have come to the Superdome.

Loyola

LOYOLA University, on St. Charles Avenue, is located in the University District of New Orleans. A modernistic Gothic-style building, the Louis J. Roussel Building, housing the communications department, takes up a full city block. A horseshoe curve further down the campus contains Marquette Hall, Thomas Hall and the Church of the Holy Name of Jesus.

The Catholic Jesuits built the university's complex of Gothic and Tudor structures between 1912 and 1914. Today, the university extends for two blocks and is operated as a private college. It offers degree programs in arts and science, business administration, dentistry, law, music and education as well as graduate studies.

Tulane

TULANE University was endowed by Paul Tulane, a New Orleans merchant, in 1884. It comprises the former University of Louisiana which dates back to the foundation of the medical college in 1834. The Sophie H. Newcomb Memorial College, the original women's department of the school, was endowed by Josephine Newcomb in 1886 and transferred to the Tulane campus in 1918.

The central building along St. Charles Avenue is Gibson Hall, built in 1894. Tilton Hall, on the left, was added

University of New Orleans

THE University of New Orleans is another of the city's institutes of higher education. In 1930, the University of New Orleans combined with Straight College to form Dillard University. Dillard was primarily a Black college for some years. In the 1970's, the university took back the name University of New Orleans. Fully integrated, the university offers degree programs to all ethnic members of society.

The university, located on the shores of Lake Pontchartrain, has a new Lakefront Arena sports and en-

tertainment facility. Its basketball team plays in the NCAA Division 1 competitions.

Although New Orleans doesn't have a major league baseball team, the University of New Orleans fields a top-flight collegiate team.

in 1901 and Dinwiddie Hall, on the right, in 1936. These buildings and those immediately behind them were built in the Romanesque style, complete with arched windows and doors.

Tulane has been referred to as the "Harvard of the South" and is well known for its excellent medical and law schools and extensive library.

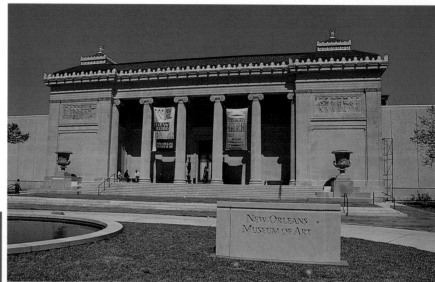

THE New Orleans Museum of Art, NOMA to locals, is a nationally recognized art museum with extensive collections of pre-Columbian, African and local arts. It also has a permanent exhibit of Imperial Treasures by Peter Carl Fabrege including three Imperial Easter Eggs once belonging to the Russian royal family.

Although the Confederate flag only flew over New Orleans for a year, the Confederate Museum, the oldest museum in Louisiana, built in 1891, holds a treasure trove of artifacts and records of the war.

The city has a wonderfully large collection of sculptural works honoring the people who shaped its history. The statue of General P.G.T. Beauregard, a Civil War hero, stands at the entrance to City Park, once the sugar plantation of Louis Allard in the late 1700's.

slang term sansfruscins, "without a penny in my pocket." The name was derived from the condition the planter found himself in after paying exorbitant construction costs. The home is very unusual.

The Houmas House Plantation in nearby Burnside got its name from the Houmas Indians who first laid claim to this point of land. The original four room house was built by Alexandre Latil in the late 18th century. Latil, with Maurice Conway, purchased the land from the Houmas. In 1812, the plantation was bought by Revolutionary War hero General

THE Great River Road stretching between New Orleans and Baton Rouge is lined with some of the finest Old South plantation homes in the country.

The twenty-eight gnarled oak trees leading to Oak Alley Plantation lend the plantation its name. The oaks were planted in the early 1700's, and the plantation house was built in 1839. A restaurant and bed and breakfast cottages are located on the grounds.

San Francisco Plantation was completed in 1856 in "Steamboat Gothic" style. The plantation was called St. Frusquin for the French

Wade Hampton. His daughter Caroline and her husband, John Smith Preston, built the magnificent Greek Revival mansion in 1840, and eventually attached the original dwelling to the house by an arched carriageway.

Once part of a hugely successful 20,000 acre plantation, Houmas House fell into disrepair in the late 1800's. In 1940, Dr. George Crozat purchased the house and set about restoring it to the grandeur it possessed in 1840.

Nottoway, built in 1849 for John Hampden Randolph, a prosperous sugar planter, brought innovative and unique construction features to the South, including indoor plumbing, gas lights and coal fireplaces. The home features 53,000 square feet of living space, enough to accommodate Randolph's eleven children.

A monument to a bygone era, the home contains wonderful examples of hand-carved marble mantels, Corinthian columns and a 65-foot Grand White Ballroom where today candlelight weddings are held.

Destrehan Plantation is the oldest plantation home left in the lower Mississippi Valley. Built in 1787 for Jean Noel Destrehan, the construction was in the simple West Indies style typical of that built by early planters. Destrehan and his brother-in-law, Etienne de Bore', first mayor of New Orleans, perfected the granulation of sugar, creating a profitable industry for Louisiana planters. Twin wings were added to the mansion in 1810, and a major renovation in 1830-40 changed the facade to Greek Revival Style.

THE huge expanse of Lake Pontchartrain measures 24 miles across. The lake accesses the Mississippi River through the Inner Harbor Navigation Canal, built in 1921.

A five and one half mile seawall system was built along the lakeshore in the 1940's by the U.S. Army Corps of Engineers. During World War II, the Army and Navy occupied the lake. In the 1950's, it was turned into residential land. Today, lakefront real estate is among the most expensive land in New Orleans.

Along the lakeshore, the University of New Orleans has built the modern Lakefront Arena. Near it is the Lakefront Airport for small aircraft. Further along Lakeshore Drive are the Mardi Gras Fountains, circular, 60-foot fountains which change from gold, to purple to green, the official Mardi Gras colors.

The Orleans Marina offers full boating facilities and the Southern Yacht Club, nearby, provides mooring for sailboats when they are not out catching the gentle breezes on the lake.

The Lake Pontchartrain Causeway connects with Interstate 12 near the suburban town of Mandeville. At 24 miles long, the Causeway has the world's longest over-water highway bridge.

ORDER FORM

If you would like to order additional copies of this book or sample some of our other fine products, please fill out the form below and mail to:

YOUR POINT OF PURCHASE RETAILER
OR
R.A.L. ENTERPRISES
Suite 136, 5000 A West Esplande Ave. • Metaire, LA 70006

TITLE		COST	QUANTITY	TOTAL
NEW ORLEANS PICTORIAL GUIDEBOOK	**64 PGS.**	**$8.95**	_____	_____
Cookin' New Orleans Style	64 pgs.	$7.95	_____	_____
Cookin' Country Cajun (Hard Cover)	64 pgs.	$9.95	_____	_____
Cookin' Country Cajun (Soft Cover)	64 pgs.	$7.95	_____	_____
Cookin' on the Mississippi (Hard Cover)	64 pgs.	$9.95	_____	_____
Cookin' on the Mississippi (Soft Cover)	64 pgs.	$7.95	_____	_____
Historic Houses of the Deep South	64 pgs.	$12.95	_____	_____
Favorite Recipes from New Orleans	64 pgs.	$7.95	_____	_____
Southern Seafood Sampler	64 pgs.	$7.95	_____	_____
Favorite Drinks of New Orleans	32 pgs.	$4.95	_____	_____
Plantation Country Guide	64 pgs.	$7.95	_____	_____
New Orleans - Birthplace of Jazz	56 pgs.	$7.95	_____	_____
New Orleans - Crescent City	32 pgs.	$4.95	_____	_____
Laminated New Orleans Placemats	Set of 4	$9.95	_____	_____
Laminated Louisiana Plantation Placemats	Set of 4	$9.95	_____	_____
Laminated Mississippi Plantation Placemats	Set of 4	$9.95	_____	_____
New Orleans Coloring Book	32 pgs.	$4.95	_____	_____
Louisiana / Mississippi Coloring Book	32 pgs.	$4.95	_____	_____
Recipe Box Cards	Set of 10	$5.95	_____	
		Postage & Handling		$2.00
		TOTAL		_____

☐ Check Enclosed   ☐ Visa   ☐ MasterCard   ☐ American Express   ☐ Discover

Card Number _____ Expiration Date _____

Name _____

Address _____

City _____ State _____ Zip _____

Daytime Phone (_____) _____

All items are satisfaction guaranteed and your purchase will be promtly refunded if returned within 30 days.
Please allow two-four weeks for delivery. No foreign orders please.